CHRISTIANS AROUND THE CLOCK

52 OBJECT LESSONS FOR CHILDREN
BASED ON THE EPISTLES

by Wesley Runk

Copyright 1971
The C.S.S. Publishing Co.
Lima, Ohio

TABLE OF CONTENTS

Are You a Missing Sleeve?	1
Life Is Like A Seed	3
The Sound of Harmony	5
Keeping on Top	7
Christians Around the Clock	9
Snapping Bak	11
Jesus Shares His Victory	13
Heaven Will Be like a Magnifying Glass	14
Practice Being Good	16
Children of the Light	18
Joined by Jesus	19
Belonging to God	21
Important People	23
Hallelujah -- Christ is Risen	24
Witnesses of Love	26
Walking in God's Way	28
Laws Are Made for Everyone	29
Making our Way Bright	31
Empty Images	33
Becoming God's Tools	35
With Many Voices	37
God Is All things for All People	39
Actions Speak Louder than Words	41
What Color Is God?	43
Exercising to Be a Christian	45

In God's Own Time	47
Why Must We Suffer?	49
The Gift of Life	51
Bringing Back the Shine	53
Christian I.O.U.'s	55
God Is like a Key	57
One with Jesus	58
God's Telegrams	59
Confident Living	60
God Keeps His Promises!	61
Separating the Good and the Bad	63
Working Together	65
Called by Name	67
Tending God's Garden	69
Becoming Clean Again	71
"Turned On" by God's Love	73
Armed with Faith	75
Sing with Joy	77
Carbon Copy Christians	78
Who's a Saint?	80
God Is like a Clock	82
Love Is like Soapsuds	84
Jumping to Conclusions	86
Why We Worship Together	88
Blueprint for Action	90
The Joy of Giving	92
Being in God's Family	94

ARE YOU A MISSING SLEEVE?

January

Romans 12:4-5   "For just as there are many parts to our bodies, so it is with Christ's body. We are all parts of it, and it takes every one of us to make it complete, for we each have different work to do. So we belong to each other and each needs all the others."

Object: Clothes with parts missing -- a pair of pants with one leg missing, one ear muff, shirt with arm or collar missing, etc.

Good morning, boys and girls, and how are you on this fine Sunday? We havn't said much about it lately but isn't it great to get together on God's day in God's house? Sometimes we may not see each other for a whole week or at least six days and then we come back together and it makes us feel good.

Say, I brought you something today that I thought all of you might be able to use. Do you know what it is that I brought? (Let them guess what you brought and when they have suggested a couple of things bring out your bag). What I have is right in here. Clothes!! Oh boy, real clothes. Now I am going to have to fit them because I only have certain sizes. Would you come up and let me see if this shirt would fit you? (Hold up shirt with no collar or sleeve.) How about you? (Call up another and try pants with no legs.) How do those pants look? Maybe you would like to wear these earmuffs and you could wear these shoes. (Pair without any soles or heels.) What's the matter, don't you like my clothes that I brought you? What's the matter with them? (Let them respond.)

Do you mean that you have to have all of the parts before they are any good? Well, I guess you are right at that!

I really did know, but the reason that I brought them is to show you something that God teaches us. He says that we are all part of Jesus' body and when one of us is missing or when one of us is not doing his job then things don't work right. When you are not here on Sunday in Sunday School and church, then our church and Sunday School look like my clothes. Something is missing and it just doesn't work right.

Do you understand what I mean? No matter how small you are or how big you are it still means that you are important.

Do you understand? I hope so. God bless you. Amen.

LIFE IS LIKE A SEED

January

Titus 3:4-7

"But when the goodness and loving kindness of God our Savior appeared he saved us, not because of deeds done by us in righteousness, but in virtue of his own mercy, by the washing of regeneration and renewal in the Holy Spirit, which he poured out upon us richly through Jesus Christ our Savior so that we might be justified by his grace and become heirs in hope of eternal life."

Object: Seeds (preferably vegetable or garden seed)

Good morning, boys and girls, and Happy New Year to you. How many of you know what year this is? (Wait for response). What's new about it? Did the world put on new clothes like a brighter sun or a bluer sky? No? Well then, what is new about it? You don't know! I'll tell you what is new, we all started over! That's right, the new year means we can begin all over so you can forget your mistakes and your broken promises and begin again.

I have something with me this morning that I saved so that it could begin again. It grew once and is now dead, but what I have will begin all over. Does that sound like a riddle? What could I have that once was part of something that lived, is now dead, but will live again?

Do you remember that God promised us that if we believe in him he will take us after we die and make us live again? How many of you remember God saying something like that?

Last summer I had some tomatoes that I grew in my back yard. How many of you know what a tomato plant looks like? It has a long stem, kind of looks like a fuzzy piece of celery and has leaves that are rough and kind of pointed in places but the best part is the round red ball that we call a tomato. Well, inside of that red ball called a tomato are seeds. Now my plants got brown and finally gray after they died and they no longer stood up but just

-3-

fell on the ground. Finally, we had to cut them up and burn them. But I kept some of the seeds and people tell me that if I plant them and water them and take care of them inside my house, those seeds that came from those dead plants will live again. God promised that it will happen too.

How many of you would like some of my seeds? Wonderful! Now you have to take good care of them just like God takes care of you. Will you take good care of them? You will, that's fine.

Someday even after we die we shall live again just like these seeds. God promised. God bless you and Happy New Year to you.

THE SOUND OF HARMONY

January

Romans 12:16a "Live in harmony with one another."

Object: Choose a live quartet from your choir and let them practice beforehand a very simple number. We want each to sing his own part and then put it together.

Good morning to you, boys and girls. Today we're going to have a great deal of fun because today some of our choir members are going to sing just for you. Do you like to hear people sing? I do too. How many of you know what the word harmony means? Well, today we are going to find out.

Now let me introduce our quartette to you. (Introduce them by name and part -- Mr. Jones, bass). Will you sing for us your tune, Mr. Bass? (Then let him sing.) That was great -- kind of low, wasn't it? (Proceed with each part this way, thanking them always by their part name). Now we are going to ask them all to sing their tune at the same time. Won't that be different? Four different parts at the same time but it is going to sound good. (Now is the time to sing the song in harmony). Wasn't that wonderful? All four songs sung together made one pretty song and I even like the one song better!

Thank you, Mr. Bass, Mr. Tenor, Miss Alto and Miss Soprano.

That is what we call harmony when we can take different tunes and put them together in one song.

That's what God asks us to do as people in his Church. He wants all of us who are different to work together in order to make one church. Now if we don't work together we will not be in harmony and we will sound terrible! But if Jane and Tom and Jan and Mike all work together, then God's Church will be in harmony. Just as the members of the quartette had to listen to the other parts, we have to live in such a way that we are listening to others so that we fit in harmoniously. We have to hear the other part if it is going to sound good. As God's people we have to first think about the other person and do what is best for him and then we will know what it means to live together in harmony.

KEEPING ON TOP

Third Sunday in Epiphany   **January**

Romans 12:21   "Do not be overcome with evil but overcome evil with good."

Object: A cork, tub, or pan of water. (It would be good to have enough small corks to pass out).

Good morning to you, boys and girls. I say that to you every week, don't I? Maybe you could help me find something new to say. In the New Testament they sometimes said, "Greetings in the name of Jesus Christ," or "Grace be to you." Well, anyway, maybe you will help me find something new to say to you.

Has anybody ever called you a cork? You heard me right, has anyone said to you, "Hi, Cork?" No? Well, that's what I'm going to call you. All of you. O.K.? "Hi, Corks.' Now let me tell you why I want to call you corks.

Do you see this big tub of water that I have? Fine. Well, now I'm going to put some corks in the water and we'll see what they do. (Empty container of corks into the water but make sure there is one big cork that all of the children can see). What are the corks doing? (Wait till someone tells you they are floating). Right, they are floating on top of the water. Now I'm going to push down on this cork and make it sink. (Act surprised when it pops back up. Do it several times). This time I'm going to hold it down until all the holes fill up with water and then it will sink. (Try that and show them that you can't sink it). Well, how about that! Maybe, that's why I want to call you corks. No matter how hard I try, I can't keep the cork down.

Right now, there are a lot of things around you that would like to make you bad. There are bad books, bad people, bad T.V. shows and a lot of other things that want to make you like them. They keep pushing you down, like I pushed the cork down, waiting and hoping that you will be bad like them. But if you are a Christian you will pop back and do something good even for those who try to hold you down. And you know what? God says that if we keep doing good to those who want us to be bad, they will someday be good too. So I want you to be like our corks and no matter what happens keep trying to be good.

CHRISTIANS AROUND THE CLOCK

February

II Corinthians 6:2 "Behold, now is the acceptable time; behold, now is the day of salvation.'

Object: A play clock, one that you can move the hands around to whatever time you want. (Can be borrowed from elementary school).

Good afternoon, happy faces. I mean good evening, no, I mean Good Morning! What time is it? Does anyone have a clock? (Look around until you find your big play clock). Oh, let's see, it's 11:00; It must be 11:00 in the morning. That's about the time when you come to church, isn't it? Good. Have you ever noticed that there is a right time to do everything? Let me show you.

How would you like to go to school at this time, 5:00? Boy, it would either be so early you would still be in bed or so late that you would be ready to eat dinner. Let's see, how would you like it if your mother told you to go to bed at this time? (Move your clock to 3:00). That would be right in the middle of the afternoon or night. Let's try one more. Suppose you had to wait till this time to eat your last meal for the day (11:00). You see, there is a right time and a wrong time for many things.

Well, that's the way it is with some things, but there is something that is right all the time. St. Paul tells us that all the time is the right time to tell the world about Jesus and tell the people how Jesus can help them.

Anytime is a good time for Jesus. Let's see what I mean. When you get up in the morning you want to thank him for the good rest you got and then a prayer of thanksgiving for your breakfast cereal, juice and toast. You want to help your friends at school because Jesus would want you to help them. There are lots of times besides these to show and tell others what Jesus means to you but this is a beginning to help you think more about it and talk about it at home. O.K. Good, God bless you. Amen.

SNAPPING BACK

February

II Corinthians 11:30   "If I must boast, I will boast of the things that show my weakness."

Object: A broken rubber band. (Have enough to pass out, but they should all be broken).

Good morning, boys and girls. How are you today? Do you know what we call this that I have in my hand? A rubber band, that's right -- almost. It's a broken rubber band. (Up to now you have held the rubber band so that the children coud not see that it was broken -- but now show them). I have a whole bunch of broken rubber bands and I'm going to give each of you one of them. I'll bet you never thought that you'd get a broken rubber band for a gift, did you? Do you know how that happened? I wanted to see where the weakest point was in every band and so I held it like this and pulled and pulled and pulled until it (Pull until it breaks) broke. The poor weak rubber band is broken right here. Now, that means that I am stronger than the rubber band, right? I found out where it was the weakest and it broke right there.

All of us have weaknesses just like a rubber band. Some of us have weak eyes and some weak legs and some weak tempers and some weak faith and wherever our weakness is, we need help.

Well, God said to St. Paul, "Don't be afraid of your weakness, but if you wish, tell others about it and then show them how I helped you." You see, the rubber band will still be good even if it's broken, because all I have to do is tie it in a knot and put it back together and it's good as new.

Sometimes, after we have broken at our weakest point, we find out how important God is and we see how perfectly God works. If you are sad, pray that God will make you happy. I even know stories about people who were sick and who were made well by God.

-11-

When God helps us over our weakness we learn to know him better, and God is always ready to give us his power when we admit to him where we are weak. A rubber band works best after it's been tied back together. You and I work better after God has come to tie up our weak points and make us strong again. Then we can really boast. Not about ourselves, but about God.

JESUS SHARES HIS VICTORY

Quinquagesima Sunday   February

I Corinthians 9:24   "Do you not know that in a race all the runners compete, but only one receives the prize? So run that you may obtain it. Every athlete exercises self-control in all things. They do it to receive a perishable wreath, but we are unperishable."

Object: Blue ribbons (a ribbon for each child)

Good morning WINNERS!!! Did you hear that? I called you WINNERS. How many of you feel as though you had won something? Do you know what you have won? Before I tell you what you have won I must give you something. When a man wins a race or a woman wins first prize at a flower show or you are first in a school art show, what do you get? (Let them guess -- some will say a trophy, others money, but someone will say a ribbon).

A Blue Ribbon. That's right. How many people can win a race or any contest? Most of the time only one person wins, but today all of you are winners. (Pass out the ribbons). Not one of you has lost. At least I don't think so. Do you know what you have won? I'm going to tell you. You have all received eternal life. Isn't that great?

How many of you love and trust Jesus even better than your best friend? You do? That's great. Well, if you do, God says that you are on his team and that since his team has won, you are all winners. That's right. Jesus died on the Cross to make all believers winners.

Now you know why you have the Blue Ribbon and while you didn't win any race all by yourself, Jesus did win it and he wants to share his win with you. That is, if you believe in Jesus Christ as your Lord and Savior. And we all do, don't we?

HEAVEN WILL BE
LIKE A MAGNIFYING GLASS

Septuagesima Sunday   **February**

I Corinthians 13:12   "For now we see in a mirror dimly, but then face to face. Now I know in part, then I shall understand fully, even as I have been fully understood."

Object: A magnifying glass and a piece of paper with small writing or a piece of equipment with a very small patent signature.

Good morning. Are there any Valentines here today Did anyone get a Valentine last week? Isn't it wonderful to know that other people like you very much! Someday, when you grow up, you will be able to choose, if you want to, one other person to share your life with and that person will be your Valentine for the rest of your life.

How many of you have ever wished you could have a crystal ball? Do you know what some people say they can do with a crystal ball? (Wait for one to tell you that they can see the future). I don't have a crystal ball but I do have something that lets you see things that you couldn't see without it. A magnifying glass. How many of you have used a magnifying glass before? Lots of you, and did you enjoy it? Let's try it once again and see how it works. Can you read this from where you are? You can't? Well, come a little closer; can you read it now? You still can't? Well, let's try this and see how it works. (Hold up magnifying glass and let as many as possible read what it says).

A magnifying glass lets us read clearly what we can only see as a blur. Well, that's kind of the way our life today is compared with what kind of life God promises for us after we go with Jesus to heaven.

-14-

We really don't understand all of the things that God promises us now, but someday we will know all that he has told us and understand it. Then we will know what God is really like and how he answers our prayers and makes life happy and heals us when we are sick.

Someday at just the right time God will show us with his own magnifying glass what our new lives are going to be like. Won't it be great when he shows us? It sure will.

PRACTICE BEING GOOD

March

I Thessalonians 4:1   "Finally, brethren, we beseech and exhort you in the Lord Jesus, that as you learned from us how you ought to live and to please God, just as you are doing, you do so more and more."

Object: A Yo-Yo

Good morning, boys and girls. Have you had your ups and downs this week? Do you know what I mean when I say that? How do you feel when you are down? (Wait for an answer -- sad, unhappy). How do you feel when you are up? (Wait again). That's right. I brought a friend of mine along today. One who is really having his ups and downs. What is like an elevator that you can hold in your hand? Do you know? How about a Yo-Yo? How many of you have played with our friend, Yo-Yo?

It's hard, isn't it? I think it's hard. Sometimes it's so hard that I feel like giving up. (Play with the Yo-Yo and get it to go up and down a couple of times before failing). How many of you have done this before? It isn't easy, is it? Would one of you like to try? (Let one try it. A child whom you know won't do it well). It is hard, isn't it? Now I think that if I couldn't do any better than I can right now I would quit. But if I knew that by practicing and practicing I would get better, then I would do it lots of times. I would do it more and more.

The reason that I told you this is because it seems that no matter how hard we try, we fail. It doesn't seem worth it to be a Christian. But you know if we try to be Christian and sin less every day, then being a Christian becomes more and more fun. Sometimes it seems that all we do is break the rules. We forget to be good to our Moms and Dads. We get angry with our brothers and sisters and we even lie to our friends. But we must keep trying by practicing to be what Jesus wants us to be.

It's just like trying to be a champion Yo-Yo player. You have to practice every day or you soon fail. We all want to be good Christians, don't we? Sure, we do, for that's the way that others come to know Christ best, when they can see him shining through you.

CHILDREN OF THE LIGHT

March

Ephesians 5:7-8 "Therefore do not associate with them, for once you were darkness, but now you are light in the Lord; walk as children of light."

Object: Piece of wood, paint brush, some oil or water base paint, some dirt or wood shavings.

Good morning, children of the light!!!! That's a new one, isn't it? Has anyone ever called you a child of light before? You know that not everyone is a child of light, don't you? You know why? Because the light isn't yours, it belongs to someone else. Do you know where the light comes from that I see in you? (See if you can't get one to say God or Jesus). Right, from God. St. Paul says that children of light should be very pleased to know that God wants to shine through them and they must or should want to live the way God wants them to live. God says that we should love everyone and be kind to all but we should choose our friends carefully.

Has your mother ever told you to pick your friends carefully because you will be what your friends are? Let me show you. How many of you like to paint? I do too, because paint always makes everything look bright and clean. Let me show you. (Take a board and paint it a bright red or blue). That's pretty, isn't it? It makes the old board look brand new and clean. Now watch what happens when we are not careful where we put the board. (Lay it in a pan of dirt or dust sufficient to pick up and mess up the paint job). Oh, that's too bad. It looks awful, doesn't it? and what are we going to do? You see, that's what happens when we aren't careful with our lives and play with people who like to get everybody into trouble.

Do you think you know what Paul means now? It's a good thing to remember what he said. We should try to help all people know about God, but we should be very careful who we choose for our best friends.

JOINED BY JESUS

March

Hebrews 9:15   "Therefore he is the mediator of a new covenant so that those who are called may receive the promised eternal inheritance, since a death has occured which redeems them from the transgressions under the first covenant."

Object: Two pieces of clothesline rope about 10" long and knots that have been tied and the ends cut off so that only the knots remain. There should be enough knots for all the children.

Good morning, boys and girls. Do you know what Sunday this is? It's Passion Sunday and to you it means that we are drawing closer and closer to what day? (Let them answer Easter). That's right, but before we come to Easter we must first learn about some other days like Good Friday. Do you know what happened on Good Friday? (Wait for 'Jesus died for us.').

I want to see if I can show you what's so important about Jesus' dying for us. Do you see these two pieces of rope? (Hold up both pieces). A couple of days ago this rope was all one piece until it was cut in half and now each piece is only half as long as the one piece was. One of these ropes I am now going to call God and the other rope man or maybe we will call it children. Now God wanted the children to be all one with him and the children wanted to be one with God but there was no way to get together.

But wait -- there was a way. God had a plan. He went to the children and took them and joined them to himself and he formed a knot. (Tie knot). He called the knot Jesus. Now, because of Jesus, God and man were back together again. Now we can see God through Jesus and God can show us how to live through Jesus.

Do you understand? You never heard of Jesus being a knot, did you? But it is a small way of showing you how important Jesus is to us if we want to be with God.

Now I have some knots for you and you take them home and put them on your dresser and you will remember how Jesus brought you back together with God.

BELONGING TO GOD

March

Galatians 4:30 "Cast out the slave and her son; for the son of the slave shall not inherit with the son of the free woman."

Object: A round hole and a square peg.

Good morning. Someone told me that you are the Lord's children. Is that right? Do you belong to the Lord? (Let them answer). What does it mean to be children of the Lord? (See if you can get several answers). Well, that's fine and I'm glad that you belong to him.

Do you know what I have here with me today? (Show them the round hole and the square peg. See if anyone can or will name the pieces). This is a round hole and this is a square peg. Do you think I can put the peg into the hole? How many of you think it will fit? (Let them hold up their hands). Let's try it. Maybe we can get the other end to fit. No, it just won't go.

You see, a square peg just won't fit in a round hole. St. Paul tries to tell us something like that when he says that some people say that the only way to get to heaven is to be real good. Paul says, the way to heaven is to believe in Jesus. There are two different thoughts and only one of them can be right. Now we have to make a choice. We must either believe that the only way to be with God is to pretend that we are as good as he is or we must trust and believe that Jesus died for the things that we did wrong. St. Paul says that they are two different things, just like a round hole and a square peg.

Becasue we are Christians, we believe that Jesus did all that was necessary for us to live with him in heaven. We know that we can never be as good as he was so we trust that he will forgive us with love and let us live with him forever.

IMPORTANT PEOPLE

March

Philippians 2:9

"Therefore God has highly exalted him and bestowed on him the name which is above every other name."

Object: Name tags and pictures of Jesus

Good morning. I have a very funny question to ask you right away. How important are you? Are you very important? What happens when you are important? (Now make comments until you get the answer that other people know you by name. Some people who are important are rich, some people important have high offices like President or Mayor or Governor). When you are important everyone knows your name. Are you important? (Take one chid and have him stand up). Everyone who knows his name hold up his hand. Lots of people know you, but not everyone. Let's try another. (Try several children). Why, I don't think all of you know my full name, do you? See, not everyone knows my name either.

I think I will give you something called a name tag and when you get back to your seat you have your mother or father write your name on it and then put it on your shirt or blouse so everyone can see it and we will all get to know each other. But before you leave I have a picture here. I want to see if everyone knows who it is. Hold up your hands if you know. (Show them pictures of Jesus). Even the adults should hold up their hands if they know. Look children! All the adults know who it is, too. Who is this? (Let them reply).

Right. Why, Jesus must be the most important person here, because everyone knows him. That's right. God made Jesus so important that no one would ever be able to forget him.

Now we know what it really is to be important, don't we?

-23-

HALLELUJAH -- CHRIST IS RISEN

Easter   **April**

I Peter 1:3   "All honor to God, the God and Father of our Lord Jesus Christ, for his boundless mercy to us, so that we have been born again, and are now members of God's own family. Now we live in the hope of eternal life because Christ rose again from the dead."

Objects: Signs of the family (perhaps you can borrow or even send away for a family crest. For the really imaginative you might design your own: ex. Bowman; the Bow -- quiver and arrows); other signs representative of a family might simply be a picture of a house (yours), dog, etc.

HALLELUJAH -- CHRIST IS RISEN -- CHRIST IS RISEN from the dead. It's Easter, boys and girls, and that means it is the most wonderful day in the whole year. Every other day is a wonderful day but this is the very best day in the whole year. Once upon a time everybody hoped and prayed that tomorrow would come and that nothing would happen but no one has had to worry since that first Easter a long time ago.

Let me show you what I mean. A long time ago people thought there was a God but they weren't really sure that he cared about them. They didn't know what God was really like. It would be like knowing you had a father but not being sure that you belonged to your Father. Do you know what I mean? Well, you want to be sure that you belong to each other, right? Pretend this picture is a picture of your house. (Hold up picture). Who lives in your house with you? Your mother? Your brother and your sister? Does your father live with you? Let's see, how many of you have a pet? A dog, or a cat, or a gold fish, or a turtle. You do? Fine! Does your pet belong to the whole family? How about your car and the T.V.? All of these things belong to the whole family.

Well, that's what happens to you and me. Because of Jesus we now know how much God our Father in heaven cares and how much he wants us to be a part of his family. Jesus became our brother so that we could also have the same Father. Jesus gave us new life, life forever, so that we don't ever have to worry about tomorrow again. From now on we belong to God's family and someday we will know everything about how we are going to live forever. But now all we have to do is trust in Jesus.

WITNESSES OF LOVE

April

I John 5:9   "We use men as witnesses in our courts, and so we can surely believe what God tells us. And God has said that Jesus is his son."

Object: A Bible and perhaps a gavel.

 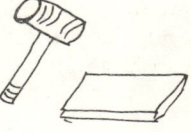

(Before you begin to talk to the boys and girls have some action taking place in front of them like an acolyte or choir member giving another member of the congregation a brightly wrapped package. Make sure that the children see this happen).

(Begin by pounding gavel on pulpit or block of wood). Order in the court!! Order in the court!! That's good, now we have order and quiet. Did you see what just happened here in front of you? How many of you saw what happened? A lot of you did. That's fine. Would you come up here, please? (Choose one of the children who raised his hand). Will you raise your right hand? Put your left hand on the Bible. "Do you promise to tell the truth, the whole truth, and nothing but the truth, so help you God?" Say, "I do."

What did you see just a moment ago before we started our sermon? (Let the child tell what he or she saw). Thank you. Who else saw what happened? (Choose another child and swear him in). Could you point out for this court who these two people were that were involved in what happened before our sermon? (Let second child answer). (Call up third child -- swear in -- ask what she saw the one person give to the other person). Thank you, you are all fine, uh, fine (pretend you can't think what to call those who testified). What do you call these people? W I T N E S S E S. That's right, witness -- a witness is someone who tells what he believes he has seen.

It is a fact that men who believed in Jesus a long time ago were called witnesses. As a matter of fact, today people are also called witnesses if they believe in Jesus. But you know what? The biggest witness of all is God the Father. That's right. Even God the Father said to all who could hear, "This is my beloved Son in whom I am well pleased." God said, "Believe in him."

All of us who hear the Word of God are asked to be witnesses of one called Jesus. If he loves you, will you tell another one about it? Good.

WALKING IN GOD'S WAY

April

I Peter 2:21b   "Follow in his steps."

Object: Some big shoes -- high heels as well as men's shoes -- size 12, 13, or 14 if possible.

Good morning, boys and girls. How are you on this fine spring Sunday morning? I love springtime and especially Sunday in the springtime. It means coming to church and singing praise to God and thanking him for the wonderful things he has done for us. It is also a time when we learn what he wants us to do.

When I was a little boy I used to do something that I know you have done. When my father came home and he was tired and he laid down on the couch, he would take off his shoes. Then I would slip over and while I still had my shoes on I would put his shoes on and shuffle around the room. How many of you girls have tried to walk in your mother's high-heeled shoes? And how about you boys? How many of you have tried to walk in your dad's shoes? It isn't easy, is it?

You find out how big your dad and mom really are, don't you? Well, I wish we could walk in Jesus' shoes. When we try to be like him, then we see how really good to us he is. When Jesus told us to love our enemies, he first showed us how to love them by forgiving them and helping them. When he asked us to help people who were sick, hungry, and without houses he did that first so that we could know how to do it.

Now St. Peter tells us that we are to walk in his steps and that means awfully big footprints, but what he means is that we should try to do what Jesus asks us to do. That means that we have to do more than wear big shoes, we have to love one another the way that he taught us to love.

LAWS ARE MADE FOR EVERYONE

April

I Peter 2:16 "Live as free men, yet without using your freedom as a pretext for evil, but live as servants of God. For the Lord's sake, obey every law of your government (those of the King as head of the state)."

Object:  Some books of law, a pair of handcuffs or a policeman's whistle.

Good morning, citizens. Have you ever been called a citizen before? (Wait for the answer). You are a citizen of your town, your county, your state, your nation. You could be called a citizen of your school or the church. It means that you are a member of a group.

What would you say makes a good citizen. (Wait for someone to say, "Obey the law"). Which law? Any law? Do you mean that if I break any law I am a bad citizen? How many laws do you think there are? Thousands, maybe millions of laws. Do you know all of them? You don't? What is going to happen when you break a law? Maybe the policeman will blow his whistle or maybe he will put handcuffs on you. Wouldn't that be awful!

Look, I have here a few books of the law and they are just a few laws of our city. There are state laws and federal laws and international laws. Now, there isn't any man who knows all of the laws, not even the very smartest judge.

And you know what? God says that we must obey all the laws. How can we do that? Do you know?

Well, God says that the best way to keep from breaking the law is to have the love which God gives you so that you can love everybody and everything. If you love the store-owner you won't steal, if you love your parents, you won't lie. If you love the other man driving his car you won't go through red lights or stop signs.

The best way for us to follow all of the laws is to first remember to love God and then we will automatically obey the law.

How many of you think you can learn all of the laws in these books today or tomorrow or a hundred years? No one. How many of you think you can share God's love with others? Everyone? That's fine.

MAKING OUR WAY BRIGHT

May

James 1:21   "So get rid of all that is wrong in your life, both inside and outside and humbly be glad for the wonderful message we have received, for it is able to save our souls as it grows in our hearts."

Object: Flashlight, some good and some dead batteries and a light bulb to put in to replace a burned out one or simply a flashlight without a bulb.

Good morning to you, boys and girls. How are you today? This is a wonderful Sunday for it is one of great joy. Do you know what we call this Sunday? It is called Cantate and it is a Latin word that means "Sing Ye" or "Sing You". We like to sing because it makes us happy. When I hear boys and girls sing I know they are happy. Do you know how I can tell when boys and girls are very sad? What do you do when you are sad? Cry. That's right.

I never hear happy children cry or sad children laugh. Let me show you something that I have with me this morning. We call this a flashlight, right? Do any of you have a flashlight? They are lots of fun, especially when it's dark and we can flash it all around the room or up at the stars at night.

I'm going to turn my flashlight on and show you what I mean. (Flick it on and off several times and show them that it doesn't work). Oh, my goodness, I wonder what could be wrong with my flashlight! Do any of you know how to fix a flashlight? What do you do? (Wait for an answer to replace batteries). I need new batteries, you say. Well, it's good that I have some with me. (Take out the old batteries and make a big deal out of getting rid of them. You might talk about gitting rid of hate, anger and things inside of us that make us sad people. They try the switch and be sad again that it doesn't work). Oh, my, now what am I going to do? I got rid of my anger and hate and prejudice but the flashlight still won't work. What else could be wrong? (See if someone talks about the bulb. If not, discover it yourself). The light bulb -- now why didn't I think of that! (Change bulb, again making a big deal of it. Discuss getting rid of the things outside that make us sinful, slapping or hitting our friends, sticking out our tongues, etc). Well, now that we've gotten rid of all the bad things like being mean to friends, and bad light bulbs, let's try our flashlight again. IT WORKS!!!!

Oh, how happy our flashlight is when it has the right things in it. It's just like you and me. When we put love inside and smiles on the outside, then we have a happy person. Isn't that great? If you do the right things outside and have good ideas inside you will shine just as bright and clear as this flashlight.

EMPTY IMAGES

May

James 1:23   "For if a person just listens and doesn't obey, he is like a man looking at his face in the mirror."

Object: A mirror (small ones for each child, otherwise, one large face mirror).

Good morning to you and to your images. Did you know that you had an image? What is your image? Have you ever seen it? Some of you have and some of you have never seen your image. (Select a child who says that he has seen his image). How many of you have ever had your picture taken by a camera? All of you have. Did you see the picture? You did? Well, then you have seen your image. It's something that looks like you, but it isn't you. Now where else have you seen your image? (talking to a child you have brought up). In a mirror? Have you seen your image in a mirror? Do you like what you see? How many children like to look in a mirror? Good. Now I'm going to try an experiment. I want you to look in the mirror. (Let him look for a second). Someone else come here and look with him. (Take two other children and let them look at themselves). Now I'm going to ask some questions and you must answer them without looking at your face. Are you ready? (Ask a series of questions, like color of eyes, hair sticking up, freckle beside nose, etc. Try to catch them each with one mistake).

You just looked at yourself, but you can't remember everything about yourself. The Bible said that you would do just that. As a matter of fact, the Bible teaches us that when people look in a mirror and then can't remember what they have seen, they are just like people who listen to God but don't obey.

Do you know what I mean? If you just listen but don't do what God says then nothing really has happened. If God tells you not to lie and you hear him teach you that but you still lie, then you haven't done right for God. If God tells you to obey your parents and you don't obey, then you have done wrong no matter how well you have listened. You have to remember what you saw in the mirror for it to do any good and you have to obey what God has told you for it to be right.

Beginning today, you must not only listen, but you must obey God as well. O.K.? God bless you.

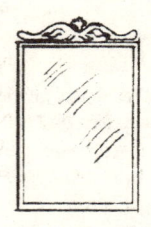

BECOMING GOD'S TOOLS

May

I Peter 4:10

"God has given each of you some special abilities. Be sure to use them to help each other, passing on to others God's many kinds of blessings."

Objects:

Hammer, nail, board, a saw and board, a screwdriver, a screw and board with a hole already made so the screw can be put in. Start with the nail hole before hand as well and the saw-cut.

Isn't this a wonderful day for all of us, boys and girls? Did you know that almost two thousand years ago Jesus' disciples began teaching people that Jesus had gone back to heaven so that everyone would be able to know about him and not just the few who lived in Israel? Aren't we glad that he did go back so that you and I can share him, like the boys and girls in Israel did a long time ago?

One of the things that Jesus teaches us today is to use our very special gifts which God gives everyone of us so that we may help others. For instance, let me show you what I have. (Hold up each tool and let them identify them). Now let me see if we can use them correctly. May I have some volunteers? Good. Now will you take this? What do you call it? A saw. That's right. Now will you take this screw and put it in this board? Will you take this hammer and cut this board in half? And would you take the screwdriver and pound in the nail? O.K.? NO? What's the matter? I never was very good with tools. Suppose you just change them around until you think you have the right ones. Wonderful! Do they work? Oh, that's fine. Do you see what we can get done when we all work together and help one another?

-35-

Well, now you know why God has made certain people to do certain things and when you do what you are able to do very well, you make the other person very happy.

That's why some people are doctors, some build houses, some grow food, others drive trucks and when all of us do our very best, then we can make each other happy. Now you should begin thinking about what you can do best and how you can make others happy.

WITH MANY VOICES

Whitsunday

Acts 2:11b "And we all hear these men telling in our own languages about the mighty miracles of God."

Objects: Bibles written in several languages with members of the congregation who can read them.

A long time ago, boys and girls, God caused a miracle to happen that men have never forgotten. It was a day something like today and all of the people who believed that Jesus was the Son of God came together to worship just as we are this morning. As they were there listening to one of the disciples preach, and they were singing some of the psalms that King David had written, something happened.

First, there was a noise like the roar of a thousand jet planes and a wind in the house like they had never seen or heard before. Then as the wind quieted, things like flames or tongues of fire danced on everyone who believed in Jesus. That in itself would be a miracle, wouldn't it? But listen to this. There were people in Jerusalem, where the disciples lived, from all over the world. People who live all over the world look like us but they do one thing differently. Do you know what that is? (Let them guess -- they speak a different language). Right. They speak differently. Well, Jesus' disciples could only speak their own language but God wanted the whole world to know about his Son. So guess what happened? See if you can guess what God did for the disciples? (Now have some members stand and read from their German, French, Spanish and Chinese Bibles). Do you know now what God did? He made a miracle happen. Each disciple spoke a language that he hadn't known before. The important thing, the real miracle was not the disciples' speaking, but that the people were hearing about Jesus in their own language for the first time, in a way that they could really understand.

Today, that same miracle happens every time a Bible is printed in a new language for people who have never heard about Jesus. We can help people hear about Jesus for the first time when we give our money to have Bibles printed.

A long time ago God caused a miracle to begin and he keeps right on having it happen everytime someone hears about Jesus for the first time.

GOD IS ALL THINGS FOR ALL PEOPLE

June

Romans 11:33   "O the depth of the riches and wisdom and knowledge of God! How unsearchable are his judgments and how inscrutable his ways!"

Object: A pocket, a big sack -- such as burlap, a book, some money, a leaf, a feather.

Boys and girls, do you know what a mystery is? Do you like mysteries? Tell me what you think a mystery is. (Allow them to give you their definitions). Well, those are all pretty good answers. I have a mystery for you today and I wonder if you might help me solve it. Let's see what I have here. It looks like a coat and in this coat is a pocket. How many of you have pockets? Wonderful, a lot of you have pockets! Now, listen to my question very carefully. Do you think God could fit into your pocket? Let's see what else I have here. (Pull out a big sack). Do you think God could fill up this entire sack so there wouldn't be any room left in it for anything else? Those are interesting questions, aren't they? Let's see what else I might have here. Oh, a rock. Do you think God is as strong and hard as this rock? Do you? How about this leaf? Do you think he is as soft and frail as this leaf?

What else do I have here? Here's a good one. Do you think that God is richer than a prince? Do you think that he is rich? They why does he need our offerings? You see what I mean about a mystery? He is small enough to fit into a pocket and that means that he could get into your heart. It also means that God can be as close as right here in church or riding in your car or he could be as far away as the moon. God is big and God is small, God is rich in some ways, but if we mean money, then he is poor. God is stronger than a rock but he is as fragile as a leaf. He is as heavy as this book or he can be as light as a feather. God is a mystery. God is everywhere and that is really why he is God. He is whatever we need him to be. If you understand that God is all of these things, then maybe you can understand why God can listen to all of your prayers, even if you all say them at the same time. You will also understand then that God thinks that you are important. You are so important that he gave you a name and asked you to be a part of his family. So the next time you wonder if God is listening to your prayers, or if he is where you are, then you can remember what you learned today. God is all things for all people.

ACTIONS SPEAK LOUDER THAN WORDS

June

I John 3:18   "Little children, let us not love in word or speech but in deed and in truth."

Object: Waste basket filled with paper and cans, dish cloth and towel, clothes and some kind of pet food.

Well, boys and girls, this morning we are going to find out some things about you. We are going to ask you some questions and see how well you do with your answers. Let me start with an easy one. How many of you love your mothers and fathers? Hold up your hand if you love your Mom and Dad. All of you do! Isn't that wonderful! I wonder what your parents would say if I asked them if you loved them? You say that you love them, but how do I know? Let's see, I have some things here that I think you probably have seen before. (Bring out the waste paper basket). Does anyone ever ask you to take out the trash? They do? Do they ever have to ask you more than once? Do you ever do it without being asked? Let's see what else I have here. What is this? (Hold up dish cloth and dish towel). How about the same questions? Do you ever do the dishes? Do you do it the first time that you are asked? Do you ever do it without being asked? Let's see what else I have. How many of you have pets? A dog? A cat? Fish? Who feeds them? Have you ever forgotten? How would you like it if your mother forgot to feed you? Do you ever have to be reminded or do you think of your responsibility before you are asked?

There are more ways of showing love than just saying, "I love you." If you say that you love God, but act like you have

-41-

forgotten him, or if you say that you love God but do things that you know God wouldn't like, then what is he supposed to think? The Bible says that what we say and what we do ought to be alike. I mean that if you love God, then you will try to do things that God wants you to do and if you don't love God then he knows why you do the things that he doesn't like. But I know you, and I know you love God like you love your Mom and Dad, but sometimes you forget. So, as you grow older, I hope that you won't forget so often and instead do the right things even when you aren't asked or even reminded.

WHAT COLOR IS GOD?

June

I John 4:20   "If anyone says, 'I love God,' and hates his brother, he is a liar; for he who does not love his brother whom he has seen, cannot love God whom he has not seen."

Object: Ball point pens or construction paper with the colors being black, brown, red, white, and yellow.

Today, my friends, we are going to learn a lesson from a question, and it is the kind of question that is troubling a lot of people. I am going to ask you a question that I want you to think about for a minute. What color is God? What color do you think God is? That is a good question. What color do you think God is? (Ask several of the children; I think you will get some surprising answers and it may also help to break the tension).

What if I asked you what color man is, boys and girls? Could you tell me what color man is? That's right, some men are black, some are white, some are red, some are tan, some are brown, some are yellow. We don't have any purple men, do we? People sometimes say the men on Mars are green, but we don't really know if there are more colors of people in God's world. Look what I have. (Hold up the ball point pens or paper). What are these? That's right, they're pens. They are all pens. Each one is a different color on the outside but they all do the same thing. We would call them all pens. Which color pen would you like if I had enough to give them away? (Let each one choose the color he would like). You don't hate any of the pens simply because they are a different color than the one you have, do you? No, you really like all of the pens, don't you? Are you still thinking about the question that I asked you in the beginning? You remember -- I asked you what color is God?

Do you think that it's possible for people to hate someone else or be afraid of someone else just because he is a different color? Jesus taught us that it would be impossible for a man to love God, whom he has never seen, if the same man hated a man that he had seen. Jesus even said something pretty strong; he said that anybody that tells you that he loves God and still hates another man, is a liar. Now we don't often call someone a liar because that is pretty strong talk. But you know there are people who hate other people just because they are a different color. Now people hate people for other reasons too, but sometimes this is one of the reasons. We believe that God even gave each one of us the color we have according to his plan.

Are you still thinking of the question that I asked you at the beginning? Do you know what color God is? I'll bet you think I have the answer. You know what? I don't know and I can't know because, like Jesus says, I have never seen God. But I know that God made some men yellow and some tan and some white and some black and some red and brown. Maybe God doesn't have any color, but we do know what he says. We should love everybody and that means caring what happens and trying to help any person who needs your help. When you love a person, whom you can see, God knows you can also love him, whom you cannot see. It surely is an interesting question, though, isn't it? What color do you think God is?

EXERCISING TO BE A CHRISTIAN

June

I Peter 5:6-11   "And after you have suffered a little while, the God of all grace who has called you to his eternal glory in Christ, will himself restore, establish and strengthen you."

Object: Some exercise equipment if available such as hand grips or jump rope or anything of that nature. Probably the most effective effort, though, would be to lead some exercises. You must divide the children into two groups.

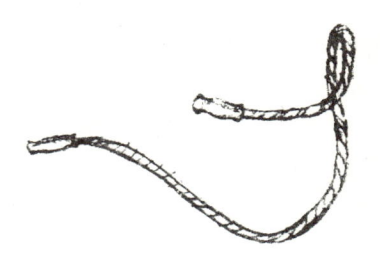

Good morning, boys and girls. How do you feel on this bright Sunday morning? Is everybody strong and healthy? Who doesn't feel strong and wide awake on a beautiful day like this? (If there is anyone who says that he is not strong or wide awake take him immediately out of the group and make him the core of your exercise group). What do you do to make yourself strong and healthy? Do you eat spinach and lots of vegetables? How many of you get at least eight hours sleep a night? Wonderful! How else do you stay so healthy? Have you ever heard of exercising? I'm going to try an experiment. Let me begin with the sleepyheads and the weak ones and take them over to this side. The rest of you can just sit there and watch what we are going to do. Now I have some exercises that I want you to follow. I am going to show you and then you are going to keep doing the exercise until I stop counting. (Have them touch their toes to a particular count. After finishing that you can have them do some others if you want, depending on your time.) That's fine, but exercises sure do make you tired. Look at the group over there that didn't do any exercises; they're not tired at all. I'll bet you wish that you had just stayed in your seat and then you wouldn't be tired. Exercise is hard work; it tests our bodies, doesn't it? But what about tomorrow? You'll be stronger than the group that didn't exercise! Right?

Well, sometimes we wonder why we should exercise when it makes us so tired, but then we find out the answer later. People ask the same question of God when they are sick or they suffer in some way that they don't understand. They say, "Why do I have to suffer, God? What did I do wrong that means that I have to feel bad today?' But God tells us that it is like a test for us and the test will make us strong so that later on when we face bigger tests we will be able to pass them and accept them. None of us likes to be sick, but we learn to be patient and to take better care of ourselves and sometimes when things happen that we don't like, we are better able to understand that Jesus is with us and will help us when we need him. So suffering a little now is like exercising. It makes us sore today, but it makes us strong tomorrow. That's a hard lesson to learn, but maybe you can talk it over with your parents on the way home and they can explain it even a little better to you.

IN GOD'S OWN TIME

June

Galatians 1:11-20   "For I did not receive it from man, nor was I taught it, but it came through a revelation of Jesus Christ.'

Object: A painting or a piece of sculpture that has been wrapped or covered with a cloth. (Most large department stores will allow you to borrow one for the purpose and in many cases will even give you an easel to display it. The brighter and more colorful, the prettier it will seem to them.)

Isn't this a lovely day, a really beautiful day? One of the things that I like about Sunday is that it brings you and me together to talk about God. Sometimes we think God is hard to know and since we can't see him we even wonder where he is. But you know, when I'm with you, I can feel God just like I can feel a warm day.

I'm sure you're wondering just what I've brought with me today. In a way, you know that I have something because you can see that something is hidden behind the piece of cloth. I mean, you know there is something there, but until that cloth is removed, you don't know what it is. This is the way an artist gets ready to show everyone his painting or that a man who makes things out of clay or metal keeps it hidden until he wants people to see it. It remains hidden until just the right time and then, when the artist chooses to let people know what he has done, he takes off the cloth.

This is somewhat the way in which God speaks to men or works for men. I want you to know that God knows what he is doing. He has the whole world planned, but some things he doesn't want people like you or me to know until just the right time. God calls that revealing himself. Can you say "reveal?" It means to uncover something that has been hidden. For instance, God was always a

God of love, but we didn't really know how much God loved us until he showed us in Jesus Christ. God revealed himself to us in Jesus. St. Paul, who wrote our lesson today, said that God revealed himself to me. And you know what? God reveals himself to you and me in special ways sometimes and we know certain things about how he loves us and why something happened that other times God will reveal himself to people like Paul and will say, "I want you to tell the whole world." Well, that's the kind of revealing that went on in our story this morning. God told something to Paul about how Jesus has come to save the whole world and God wanted Paul to tell the whole world about it.

Now you are probably wondering what I have to reveal to you this morning that's all covered up. Right? Well, the time is almost right -- I mean I have to wait for fifteen more seconds before I can show you, so the time will be just right. You want to help me count? Fifteen, fourteen, thirteen (count it down to the point of zero and then pull off the covering and they will see the brightest, prettiest picture that they have ever seen). Isn't that beautiful, boys and girls, and wasn't it exciting to see? Now you must know how it feels to have God reveal himself to you in such an exciting way. Because of the story you have just heard, maybe you will wait for God to speak to you like he did to Paul and then maybe you will learn something so important that God will ask you to share it with everybody in the whole world.

THE GIFT OF LIFE

July

Romans 6:19-23 "For the wage paid by sin is death, the present given by God is eternal life in Christ Jesus our Lord."

Object: A paycheck or pay envelope and a present (gift-wrapped)

Good morning to all of the beautiful children and that means good morning to all of you. That's right, you are all beautiful children because that's the way God made you. You'll never guess what I have here with me today, because, probably, none of you has ever had one. Just to be sure, let me check. Do any of you work on the railroad? Do any of you work at the grocery store? Do any of you have a job that pays money every week in the form of a pay check? None of you? Some of you work around the house and you get money from your parents for doing that work, is that right? Well, that's kind of like a pay check. You have to work for every cent you get. That's the way that most people like your dad and mom get paid. If they work forty hours, they get paid for forty hours. Whatever they earn, they get to keep. Jesus tells us that we get paid for our sins just like that. He means that because we sin we earn the punishment that is coming to us for the things that we think and say. Sounds bad, doesn't it? I mean if someone is going to punish me for all the things I do that are bad, I'm going to have a very big pay-check.

Now I want to show you something that you'll recognize. What is this that I have? (Hold up gift-wrapped package). A present. All of us like presents because they remind us of good times and because we know that we do not have to work or pay for presents. They are free and they are given to us by our friends and our family. People who love us give us presents. Jesus says that God gives us a gift. It has to be a gift because all of the money in the world or all of the hard work can't earn or buy it. It's called forgiveness and that gift of forgiveness also means that we can live forever with God and other people who love Jesus and are forgiven. Do you see

51-

what I mean? Sin is like a pay-check -- you have to work for it and you get it all by yourself but forgiveness is like a gift because God gives it freely to all who love him.

BRINGING BACK THE SHINE

July

Romans 6:3-11   "We must realize that our former selves have been crucified with him to destroy this sinful body and to free us from the slavery of sin."

Object: Rust on any object and some sandpaper (better have a large towel or some newspaper to collect the rust).

I have something with me this morning that all of us have seen before and I want you to take a good look at it. It's something that happens to your favorite toys, your dad's automobile, and other things that mean a lot to us. When it happens, we feel bad about it. Have you ever left a toy that you liked very much (like this toy truck) out in the yard and it rained and you forgot all about it and then one day you saw it and it was covered with (let them supply the word "rust")...Rust, that's right, rust. It sure is hard to imagine that one day that truck was bright and shiny and just as pretty a toy as you could have had. Now it looks bad, and hardly worth anything. But look what happens when I take the sandpaper that I have here and start to rub the rust. It comes off, and while the paint isn't there anymore like it once was, the metal is starting to shine and if I wanted to repaint it I think it would be as good as new and maybe even better.

That is kind of like the way we are, God says. When he made us originally he made us perfect, bright and shiny. But as we grow up we sin here and there and while we don't think it will hurt us much at the time we soon begin to look pretty bad to ourselves, to say nothing of how we look to God. But then we think that we had better take a better look and begin to ask how Jesus wants us to be. It's kind of hard to work or play or do anything when you're rusty or fulled with sin. You just get slower and slower and feel worse and worse. At first when God comes into your life it may be a little rough, he may even feel like sandpaper as he gets you to stop doing the wrong things that you've been doing. But then, in a little while, we're not quite so rusty and we're able to move better and better and the first thing you know, we've put our lives in the hands of God and we feel free. We can play and work much better because we're not covered with sin and what we thought was like sandpaper is now smooth like the love of God. Only Jesus can clear us up and keep us from getting rusty. It may seem kind of rough at first having your sins taken away, but in time it will make you feel like a brand new person.

CHRISTIAN I.O.U.'s

July

I Peter 3:8-15a   "Never pay back one wrong with another, or an angry word with another one; instead pay back with a blessing. That is what you are called to do so that you inherit a blessing yourself."

Object: I.O.U.'s written on paper.

I have some things with me this morning that are really going to be fun to give to you. As a matter of fact, I've been working on them all week and I've waited and waited for Sunday to come so that I could give them to you. I want to give them to you because I think that maybe you will understand Christianity a lot better when you see what I have to give you. (You will have to have enough I.O.U.'s for each child and make sure that they are things that you can do when you see one of the children either there or after church or when you call or whenever you see them. My suggestion is something like a piggyback ride for the youngest, a story that will make them feel good, a joke that will make them laugh, a prayer to make them well, a walk around the block with them, etc.). Now I want you to think real hard about something that you did that was wrong. Can you remember what you did that made someone very unhappy? Perhaps you hurt a sister or brother or told a lie or picked your mother's favorite flower, or forgot to pick up your clothes, or something like that. Do you remember something that you did that was bad? You do? Will you tell me what you did that you should not have done, and then I'm going to give you something for that. (Get a story from one of them). Oh, that was bad. What do you think I should give you for that? A spanking, or a very stern talk? Maybe I should send you to your room or make you eat only bread and water. I'm not going to do any of those things. Instead I'm going to give you this piece of paper and it has something written on it and the next time you see me I'll do whatever it says on the paper.

Shall we read this one? These are called Christian I.O.U.'s. Let's see, this one says, "I owe you a walk around the block together and a promise to listen to whatever you want to talk about. O.K., now the next time you see me near your house, you can collect that Christian I.O.U. You see, a Christian never hits back when somebody hurts him or tells a lie about somebody just because they lied about him. A Christian never does anything bad to get even, he always tries to do something that is good for the other person because he knows that this is the way that Jesus would do it for him. God always gives men a blessing, a happiness to those whom he made, and he hopes that you will do the same. If you like the way things happen to you with your I.O.U. then maybe you will want to do this for someone who has done something bad to you. And do you know what? When you do something nice to someone who has done something bad to you, the next time he will probably do something nice for you instead of something bad.

GOD IS LIKE A KEY

August

I Corinthians 10:13   "No temptation has overtaken you that is not common to man. God is faithful and he will not let you be tempted beyond your strength, but with the temptation will also provide the way of escape, that you may be able to endure it."

Object: Padlock and key, box or something to which you can attach a padlock to hold it fast.

Well, here we are, boys and girls, getting ready for the last month of vacation. It's funny how we get into things so easily and then they are so hard to leave. I know that I sure like to start my vacation and I sure am sorry when it's over. You know, that's almost the way it is with sin. You know what I mean. It's so easy when we start, but it becomes so hard when it's over.

Let me show you what I mean. You see this box? It has some of my very favorite things in it. (Just show it to a few now). Look, here is my best pen, a picture of my father and mother, a pair of sun-glasses, some bubble gum and lots of other things. It's so precious that I keep it locked up like this. (Close the lid and snap the padlock). Oh, some of you didn't get to see my favorite things.

Would you mind passing this box over so the others can see what I had? (Just pretend that you don't notice that it is locked and let them struggle to open it or wait until someone reminds you that they need the key). Oh, you can't get it open? You need the key? Why, of course you do. Here's the key. Can you open it now? Fine. That reminds me of what I wanted to tell you this morning. God is like a key. That's right. No matter what kind of trouble you get into he will always promise to get you out if you really are sorry and you want him to help you.

Isn't that great? God is like a key. He can get anyone out of anything if they love him and are sorry about getting into trouble. Isn't that great! God is like a key.

ONE WITH JESUS

August

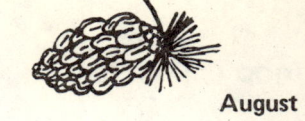

I Corinthians 12:3 — "Therefore I want you to understand that no one speaking by the Spirit of God ever says, 'Jesus be cursed!' and no one can say, 'Jesus is Lord' except by the Holy Spirit."

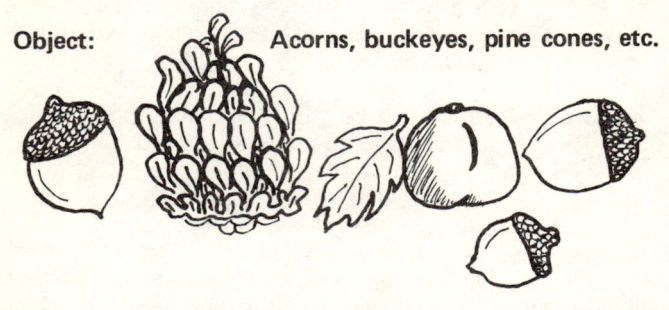

Object: Acorns, buckeyes, pine cones, etc.

Good morning, children, and how are you today? I have some things with me today that all of you have seen before and most of you like. Take a look at these and tell me what they are when I hold them up. (Then take each fruit or seed and hold it up for the children to identify). That's very good, and that means that each one of these is different from the other, and they all come from different -- what? Where do these things grow? Trees, that's right. Apple trees, pear trees, buckeye trees, pine trees and where do acorns come from? Oak trees!!! That's right.

Can an acorn come from a pear tree or a pine cone from an apple tree? Of course not! Well, in a way that's what St. Paul is telling us today in his letter to the people of Corinth. He is saying that no one who calls himself a Christian could ever curse Jesus because Christianity and cursing just don't go together. Neither can someone who is not a Christian call Jesus, Lord, because if they don't believe in him they can't know him. You see, all of these fruits come from trees, but only one tree and one fruit go together.

You children need to remember that you know that Jesus is Lord and God because you belong to him. Isn't that great! I think so and so did St. Paul.

GOD'S TELEGRAMS

August

I Corinthians 15:3   "For I delivered to you as of first importance what I also received, that Christ died for our sins in accordance with the scriptures."

Object: Idea of a messenger -- some Western Union Telegrams, copy for each child.

Today is the right kind of a day for you and me. There's no question about it, this day was meant to be shared by us. I don't think that it was an accident that you and I met together in church today. As a matter of fact, I feel like a telegram and you are the people that the telegram is being sent to. Did you ever think of the Pastor or your Sunday School teacher as being like a telegram? (Hold up telegram). Well, that's what we are, telegrams. Do you know what is in a telegram or on a telegram? (See if you can get the word "message" from them. Some say words). WORDS, that's right and what do we call it when we put the words together -- a sentence and what is another word for sentence when it is sent? A message. That's right. Do you know who is sending you a message today? God. That's who is sending you a message and instead of writing it out in a letter or putting it in a telegram he sends pastors and teachers to people so they can deliver his message for him. I like being a telegram for God and delivering his message. Would you like to know what God has told me to tell you? He told me to tell the children that Jesus died for their sins just like the Bible says.

Maybe, when you grow up God will ask some of you to be telegrams for him and then maybe some of you will be pastors and Sunday School teachers too.

CONFIDENT LIVING

August

II Corinthians 3:4   "Such is the confidence that we have through Christ toward God."

Object: Rabbit's foot, penny, four leaf clover, or a lucky stone.

Good luck, boys and girls. Do you ever wish people good luck? Do you know what luck is? Let me show you what some people believe in as luck. Here is a rabbit's foot. Do any of you have a rabbit's foot? Do you believe that a rabbit's foot can make things happen? How about a lucky penny or a four-leaf clover? Can you believe that people actually think that these things really make things go better?

You know, this idea didn't just start. People used to have little statues in their houses and they believed in them like God. But St. Paul says that there is only one person you can really have confidence in and that is Jesus Christ. Since he was the one who made things, he is also the only one who can change things. That's right. Jesus made rabbits and copper for pennies, and he made four-leaf clovers, and if he made them then you want to believe in him. St. Paul calls it confidence which is another word for believing. Can you say confidence? That's right. And when we have confidence in what Jesus tells us about God and how he loves us and cares for us then we can say that we really believe in God and then we don't need all of those other things. Jesus is enough and we have confidence that Jesus will always help us.

GOD KEEPS HIS PROMISES!

August

Galatians 3:19   "Why then the Law? It was added because of transgressions, till the offspring should come to whom the promise had been made."

Object: A contract, a marriage license, a certificate of ordination, baptismal certificate, etc.

Well, good morning to you, boys and girls. Isn't it great that vacation is over and school will soon be back in session! Pretty soon you'll be back with friends whom you haven't seen all summer. Do you remember all of the things that you were going to do that you didn't get done? Maybe you promised your friends that you would call them, or maybe even write them a letter.

Promises are really something. Let me show you some promises. Here is a promise that we call a contract. This contract is signed by two people, the man who sells and the one who buys and they promise each other things like how much they will pay and when. And the seller tells when he will deliver the item and how long it will last. That promise is a contract. Here is a promise that someday most of you will make. Do you know what this is? It's a marriage license (certificate) and it has in it a promise for two people to keep whether they are rich or poor, sick or healthy and so forth. That is also a promise that people make. Then there is another promise that a pastor makes. This promise tells everyone that he will serve God and God's church. This promise is called an ordination certificate and is very important to every pastor. Let me show you another promise that someone made to God for you. When you are baptized your parents make a promise to God that they will bring you to church and teach you about him.

Well, since we make all of these promises to God and to each other, then I wonder if God ever made a promise to us? Do you think God ever made you a promise? You're right. He made lots of promises and he has kept every one of them too. But his biggest promise of all was that he would send us a baby named Jesus who would be Christ our Lord. That's right, a long time before Jesus was even born he promised men that someday he would send his very own Son. What a wonderful promise he made! And he kept it! I hope that you can keep your promises to God as well as he keeps his promises to you.

SEPARATING THE GOOD AND THE BAD

September

Galatians 5:16-24
Vs. 17
"For the desires of the flesh are against the Spirit, and the desires of the Spirit are against the flesh, for these are opposed to each other to prevent you from doing what you would."

Object: Some cooking oil and tap water and a large clear glass into which they can be poured. The water should not be ice water and it is better if you don't shake it too hard because it takes a while for it to separate but you should shake it a little to prove your point. By the way, be sure the color of the oil is distinguishable.

Good morning to you, fellow scientists. Isn't it a wonderful day to conduct experiments? How many here like to work experiments? Wonderful! Before we make the experiment, I want to show you what we have. Here is a bottle of oil, "cooking oil," like your mother uses when she bakes a pie or french fries potatoes. Now for our experiment we are going to call the oil SELFISHNESS, DRUNKENNESS, STEALING AND HATE (you might have this written on a piece of paper and pasted over the label). How many people here want to drink a whole bottle of this? Now I have another bottle and in this bottle is pure water. Lovely, clean water that comes from your faucet. Let's see what the label says for our experiment. Why, it says LOVE, JOY, PEACE AND KINDNESS. That sounds much better, doesn't it? You know what I think I'm going to do? I'm going to ask two people to help me with our experiment. John, will you pour some hate, selfishness, stealing and drunkenness into this large glass? That's fine. Now, Susan, will you pour some love, joy, peace and kindness in the same glass so that we can mix them up? That way nothing will be all good or all bad, right? This glass will be a mixture of the two.

Oh, for heaven's sake, look at what's happening. The oil and the water are separating. They're coming apart and the oil is on the top and the water on the bottom.

You know, God said that good and evil don't belong together. God is always trying to help us see that when we hate we can only do terrible things and that nothing good comes from hate. He also told us that when we love we do only good and that when we are like that we are like him.

Now maybe you can remember to love all of the time because it's the best way to do good things.

WORKING TOGETHER

September

Ephesians 4:11 "And his (Jesus) gifts were that some should be apostles, some prophets, some evangelists, some pastors and teachers for the equipment of the saints, for the work of the ministry, for the building up of the body of Christ."

Object: If possible contact a doctor's office and see if you can borrow a plastic hand or heart that shows the make-up of that part of the human body. If it comes apart, all the better. If not, use such objects as the tools for building, like trowel, bricks, nails, hammer, etc.

Today, my friends, we have a very special lesson because it is about us and how we help to make God's Church a wonderful place for everybody to belong. But first I want to show you something about yourself. Have you ever seen what a heart (or hand) looks like under your skin? (Take the object apart if possible and show the children). It doesn't look much like a heart or hand when you take it apart does it? It's just pieces and this way it can't do a very good job for you, can it? But look again at what it looks like when we put it back together. Now it looks like a heart (or hand). Now it can do a job.

Well, God's Church is like that. When we take God's church apart we have a lot of pieces. Here we have a pastor, who is just one man with nobody to care about or preach to. Here we have a teacher, with no children to teach, and then we have an organist without an organ and a singer without music and no one to sing to and so on. (Have each person stand and call him by name. As you call each name, have that person move away from where he is located, such as choir loft, pulpit, organ, etc.).

To make God's church all of God's people must work together just like this heart or hand.

-65-

God's church is not just the pastor or priest or teacher, but it is made up of everyone who loves God and listens to him speak. Now maybe you will listen and hear what God wants you to do in his church.

CALLED BY NAME

September

Ephesians 4:1-6
Vs. 4
"There is one body and one Spirit, just as you were called to the one hope that belongs to your call."

Object: Telephone, letter (addressed to someone)

Good morning, boys and girls. It's a fine morning, isn't it? Have you noticed what is happening outside about this time of the year? Have you noticed anything beginning to change in God's world? (Let them talk about the grass being brown, the days getting shorter, the trees getting new color, etc). It's wonderful how God speaks to his world, isn't it?

I have something here that everyone knows about. (Hold up telephone). This telephone speaks too, doesn't it? Well, at least it carries your voice when you speak to another person, doesn't it? Let me ask you some questions about making a phone call. What do you say when you make a call? What is the first thing that you say? (Let them say hello). That's right, you say "Hello, this is Jimmie or Susan or Billy (use names of children who are present). That's right, you tell the person who answers your name so that he knows who is calling and then what do you say? (See if you can get someone to say that you ask for the person that you are calling). You say, "Is Mike or Janet or Fred at home?" It's important that you know who you are calling. It wouldn't make much sense to say, "Hello, I'm Jim. I want to talk." You want to talk to someone or call someone special.

Well, God made kind of a phone call when he asked you to be a Christian. He gave you a name and called you by that name and said that from now on you belonged to him. Isn't it wonderful that God knows you so well that he gives you a Christian name and makes you a member of his family, God's family!

-67-

Now you know that God did not just say, "I want some boys or girls or some friends" but he said that he wanted you and he called you to be his very own.

When you make a phone call you ask for a person by name and when God called you he did the same thing. I think that's wonderful! Don't you?

TENDING GOD'S GARDEN

September

Galatians 5:25-6:10
Vss. 6:9, 10

"And let us not grow weary in well-doing, for in due season we shall reap, if we do not lose heart. So then, as we have opportunity let us do good to all men, and especially to those who are of the household of faith."

Object: A hoe, hose, insect spray, etc.

Good morning, boys and girls. How are you on this beautiful day? Did any of you work in your gardens this summer or did you watch what kind of work your mother and dad did in their gardens last summer? Do you remember how they planted their seeds and plants? Then what did they do? Do you remember how they hoed, and sprayed and hoed some more? Do you remember how hard they worked? And they didn't get anything out of the garden during all that time? Do you remember when the tomatoes were green and there were no kernels on the corn and no peas in the pod? But do you also remember that they kept on hoeing and spraying and watering the plants even though they didn't get to eat anything?

Well, St. Paul says, that the same thing is true for Christians when they do good. Sometimes we wonder why we should keep on doing good things when it doesn't seem to help us at all. I mean, you wonder why you should tell the truth or help carry heavy packages for your mother or help your dad when you want to go out and play. But St. Paul says that we should do it because, just like your garden ripened and you ate from it, so someday all of the good things will be honored by God.

I know that you wonder how often you should have to do these things but you must always do what is right because then everybody is helped and your friends will be grateful for you.

Will you remember what I said? I know that someday you will be pleased that you did. Just remember that doing good things for people is like keeping weeds out of the garden when the seeds and plants are still growing. It might be hard work at the time but eventually you will be a lot happier with what results you get from your hard work.

BECOMING CLEAN AGAIN

October

Ephesians 4:22,23   "Put off your old nature which belongs to your former manner of life and is corrupt through deceitful lusts and be renewed in the spirit of your minds."

Object: A bucket of mud, pan with clean water, towel and washcloth and bar of soap (maybe some long aprons would be advisable).

Good morning to all of the clean people. How many of you are bright and clean this Lord's Day! Isn't it wonderful to take a bath and get all cleaned up on Saturday night so that you feel clean all over on Sunday morning?

Would you believe me if I told you that I brought a bucket of mud for somebody to play in this morning? How many of you would believe that? Well, I did and I need a volunteer who really wants to get dirty. Now you put your hands into this bucket of mud and just squish your fingers all through it. That's fine. Isn't it fun to play in the mud! That's good. Now I want you to let it dry on your hands while I explain something to the other boys and girls.

I want everybody to think of those muddy hands as being the way we are before we know Jesus. It seems natural and not too bad until we look around at other people and we notice that they're not dirty.

Suppose we want to get rid of the mud and have clean hands. What should we do? Maybe you can just rub some of it off by yourself. Rub your hands together real hard and see if they get clean...They don't, do they? Maybe someone else could help you, like your friend here. (Get a second one up and let him or her wipe off the dirty hands). Oh my heavens, now your friend is dirty too.

Well, what shall we do? I know, let's use soap, water, wash cloth and towel. Especially soap. If you use water, wash cloth and towel and your hands are really dirty, then you won't get them clean, but when you use soap let's see what happens.

Soap does for your outside what Christ does for you inside, no matter how dirty you are. It's like being made new again and getting rid of the old sin.

That's what St. Paul teaches us when he tells us to get rid of our old nature (the mud) and put on the new (our clean hands). It sometimes seems like fun to sin but when we are stuck with it and there's no way to get rid of it except through God's forgiveness, we are glad for our new beauty just like we're glad for our clean hands.

"TURNED ON" BY GOD'S LOVE

October

I Corinthians 1:9   "God is faithful, by whom you were called into the fellowship of his Son, Jesus Christ our Lord."

Object: Floor lamp with a large center (3 way) light and smaller lights around it.

Good morning, boys and girls. How are you today? Don't you think that fall weather is really beautiful -- when the air seems so fresh and crisp and the sky seems extra blue? It really is something the way God has our world planned with seasons and how they change in such wonderful fashion.

I have a lamp here with me this morning that looks a lot like other lamps you have seen, but I hope that it tells a story that will show you how we are a part of God's wonderful plan. In the center there is a large light and when we turn it on it shines brightly. Let's suppose that this big light is God. You can imagine what happens when you turn this light on in a dark room. What happens when you turn a light on in a dark room? (Wait for children to respond). It gets light, that's right. Almost all of the darkness is gone but there may be some shadows here and there.

But look at this lamp -- it not only has one big bright light, it also has some little lights around it. Do you know who the little lights remind me of when I see a light like this? (Let them guess).

They remind me of you and me. That's right. Let's call this whole

-73-

lamp "God's Kingdom" and the light God and the little lights you and me. When God calls us, that means he makes us a part of his kingdom or family. He turns us on and we become in many ways like him. We can even shine through the power he gives us.

The Bible talks about us as being in fellowship with Christ. That means that we are turned on with Christ. That means that we are turned on with him, doing the things that he wants us to do and just enjoying the time we spend together. Like right now. We are in fellowship with God and our faces should be and are as bright as the lights.

It's a nice lamp that tells us how close we are and how God wants us to be with him. But being with God is even better than being a light. We, because we are Christians, are in fellowship with God.

ARMED WITH FAITH

October

Ephesians 6:11   "Put on the whole armor of God, that you may be able to stand against the wiles of the devil.'

Object: A football uniform and all of the protective gear worn underneath it.

Good morning to you, boys and girls, and how are you on the last Sunday in October? There's a very special day coming this week that I know you're all looking forward to for a lot of fun. Do you know what day it is that I'm talking about? Hallowe'en, that's right.

One of the real fun things about Hallowe'en is dressing up in a costume so that you will look like something that's very unreal, such as a ghost or a witch or something very funny like a big-toothed rabbit. But sometimes you dress up like a person who does special things like a football player. A football player makes me think of a Christian because of a very special passage that Paul writes in his letter to the Ephesians. In that Bible passage Paul says that a Christian ought to put on things like swords and helmets and special shoes and other things like a soldier wore in the days when Paul lived.

Well, a football player today must wear a lot of things to protect himself in a rugged game of football. He must wear hip pads, and shoulder pads and rib pads and special shoes with cleats and special pants and a shirt with a number on it and a helmet. Now when a football player goes out and plays the game, he wears these things so he won't get hurt but can win the game.

We think that if a Christian puts on prayer (knee pads with word "prayer" written on tape and put on it), faith (hip pads with word on tape), love (rib pads), joy (on helmet), he is putting on his armor against the sin in the world. If every Christian dressed like this he could always win the game of life that he plays against the

-75-

devil, and I don't mean the one you'll see on Hallowe'en.

It's up to all of us to protect ourselves with the things that God gives us, like prayer, faith, love, and joy, just as a football player wears his special uniform. So let's remember what we as Christians need to play the game and play it well.

SING WITH JOY

October

Ephesians 5:18b,19   "But be filled with the Spirit, addressing one another in psalms and hymns and spiritual songs and singing and making melody to the Lord with all your heart."

Object: Hymn book and a very bright song or short anthem of praise by the choir.

"Greetings in the name of Christ," boys and girls. "Peace be with you." Those are a couple of the things that people used to say and, in some places, still say when they see each other during the day. Have you ever thought how wonderful it might be to be out in a field or meadow, and while you were waiting with your very favorite friend you could sing and talk about Jesus?

Did you know that we have a whole book of songs about God just like the Bible says we should have? That's right, the Bible tells us that we should say hello to one another in the name of Jesus and that we should also speak psalms and we have psalms right here in our book. St. Paul also tells us in the Bible that we should sing psalms to one another and we have a lot of those, don't we? In this book we have 602 hymns (insert correct number) and all through our service we sing back and forth to one another. But today we are going to let you sing a special song and then we'll see if anybody sings back to you. (Have the children sing "Praise Him, Praise Him -- All ye little children" or any appropriate hymn. When the children have finished, let the choir stand and sing one verse of a very bright hymn in response).

Wasn't that wonderful? You sang a song like Paul said you should and the choir sang right back.

When we talk or sing or read about God we are more apt to do the things he teaches us and the more we do sing and talk about these things the more we do the good things that God wants us to do.

CARBON COPY CHRISTIANS

November

Philippians 3:17-21 "Keep on imitating me, all of you. We have set the right example for you, so pay attention to those who follow it."

Object: Carbon paper and two sheets of white paper and a ball point pen.

Good morning, boys and girls! I have a question right away for you today. Do you know what the word "imitate" means? It means to try to do something just like someone else has done it. You can imitate me if you want to. Watch me and do everything that I do (Raise your right hand, then wait for them to do it -- smile and wait for them to smile or close your one eye, etc). Why, that's fine. You know what it is to imitate now, don't you?

Now sometimes you will be the leader and other people will imitate you and sometimes you will imitate others. But we must always be sure that we are imitating people who do right and we must be careful that the people who imitate us, see us doing right.

Let me show you what I mean. Here are two pieces of paper. (Have them paper-clipped together with carbon in between). Now when I write the word K A T (let the children notice that you have the mistake in spelling and then ask them to correct you). Oh, you mean that I made a mistake? Well, how do you spell cat? C A T.

Well, there, that looks better, doesn't it? I can just erase this and no one will ever know that I made a mistake. (Separate pages and erase the front page mistake. You can have the second paper titled "My Friend". Show them the corrected page). Oh my heavens, look at the piece of paper that I had under the font sheet. It has the mistake on it too, so it was wrong when it imitated me. My, we must be careful when people are following us, must we not?

If you wanted to imitate someone, who would you choose? Jesus? Maybe Peter or St. Paul? It's a good thing to pick out one of Jesus' best disciples and follow him.

That's what St. Paul said when he talked to the people in Philippi. He said, "Keep on imitating me, brothers, all of you." If you want to be a Christian leader, then you have to be sure of what you do. If you want to be a Christian follower, then you have to be careful whom you choose to follow!

WHO'S A SAINT ?

November

Rev. 7:9, 10   "And behold, a great multitude which no man could number, from every nation, from all tribes and peoples and tongues, standing before the throne and before the Lamb, clothed in white robes."

Object: Picture of Washington, Lincoln, Nixon, Martin Luther King, etc.

Good morning, boys and girls. There's something good about November. It makes you think about Thanksgiving and the reason why we're glad to be Americans. Speaking of Americans, can you tell me the name of a famous American? (Someone will reply George Washington and you can either show a picture or take out a dollar bill).

That's right, George Washington was our first President and we have his picture right here in front of us on a dollar bill. What other American do you know? Abraham Lincoln. That's right, and who's our President now? My, you know lots of famous Americans, don't you? All of them are very famous.

Let me see now how smart you really are. Can you name for me a saint in the Christian Church? Someone whom you've heard called a saint. St. Peter, why he was one of Jesus' deciples. And St. Mark, why he wrote one of the books in the Bible, and St. Paul was both an apostle of Jesus and a writer. Why, you know lots of famous Christians too.

But do you know what? You forgot to tell me the name of an American and a Christian saint that you know better than anyone else.

Do you know whom you forgot to mention? You don't know?

If you asked me to name an American I could say -- me or you --

-80-

Susie, Tom, Jack, Jane, right? Maybe we're not famous, but we are all Americans, because we were born here, because our parents are Americans, because we accept the American flag as our flag. All of these reasons make us Americans.

Now let me see if you understand. You also forgot to tell me the name of a Christian saint whom you know best of all.

You! That's right! Bill, Becky, Pam -- all of you are saints. Do you know why? The word saint means someone who believes that Jesus is God's Son and lives the way he believes. We are Christians, and because we are Christians we are all saints in Christ. We believe in the Father, Son, and Holy Spirit. We believe that Jesus died for our sins and we believe that he rose again from the dead.

You may not be famous, but you are still a saint as God sees it. Are you happy about that? I hope so.

GOD IS LIKE A CLOCK

November

II Peter 3:13   "But according to his promise we wait for new heavens and a new earth in which righteousness dwells."

Object: A large clock, preferably one with an audible tick-tock and one from when the back can be removed so that the workings can be seen.

Good morning, boys and girls. Say, that's the same thing I said last Sunday and the Sunday before that. But I like to say "Good Morning", even if it is the same. I keep thinking that I probably sound like this clock, always saying the same thing. Can you hear the clock? Listen -- tick-tock, tick-tock, tick-tock!

What a lazy old clock we have when it only goes tick-tock. It doesn't do anything else. You know, boys and girls, that's the way some people feel about God. He seems to do the same thing every day. Do you know what I mean? He hangs out the sun every morning and the moon and stars every night. He makes the wind blow, the snow fall, and he causes things to grow. He's kind of like the clock, doing the same thing every day. It doesn't sound very exciting, does it?

Did you know that people had these same thoughts years ago, even when Jesus was a boy? But you know that one of Jesus' disciples, named Peter, listened to God very closely and showed us hard God works for us. Let me show you what I mean.

When you look at the face of the clock it seems like it's hardly moving and it makes the same slow sound every time, tick-tock, tick-tock.

Now let's turn the clock around and take off the back. Look at all of the different parts and see how they move. It certainly doesn't look like what we see all the time when we look at the face of the clock, does it?

Well, this is kind of the way God is at work. We don't always know what he's doing or why he's doing it, but we can always be sure that he's working for us. He answers our prayers and helps us through each day. He heals us when we're hurt and teaches us how to love. God does everything and while we can't see him, just like we can't see the back of the clock, we know that he's always working for us and one day, when he is ready, God will have us live with him in a special place he is always getting ready for us.

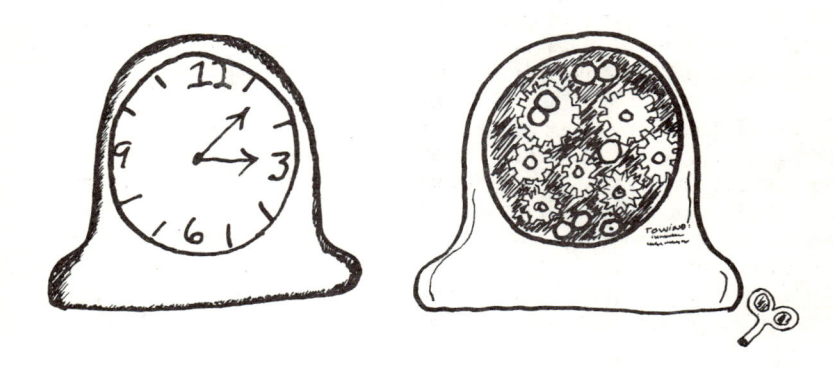

LOVE IS LIKE SOAPSUDS

November

Philippians 1:9   "I pray that your love will keep on growing more and more, together with true knowledge and perfect judgment, so that you will be able to choose what is best."

Object: Liquid detergent, glass bowl and water.

Good morning, boys and girls. Aren't the trees beautiful now that they've all changed their colors? Isn't it wonderful the way God has a plan for his whole world and all that lives in it?

Our God certainly knows what to do and when to do it. When it begins to get warm, he puts the leaves on the trees so that we can have shade, and when it gets cold and the trees need to rest, he lets the leaves fall so that the sunshine can get through. Isn't it wonderful to have not only a smart God but a God who does things on time? How many of you knew that God was so smart? All of you knew that. How many of you knew that he always does things in just the right way? You all knew that too? Terrific!

Do you know why he's so good to you and me and does these things so well? Because he loves us so much. He keeps loving and loving and loving and the more he helps, the more he loves. Let me show you.

You see this bowl of water? Well, I'm going to pour some liquid detergent into it. (Pour a generous portion but don't pour so much that it begins to make suds). When I do this, you see a few bubbles, almost as if they were an accident. This is how some people are, who know we should love everybody, but only actually try to do so once in a while.

Now if I begin to stir it up, I get a few suds; at least, you can be sure there's soap there. This is like a lot of Christians I know who are kind and loving to the people they see a lot and know pretty well. (Stir it until you can see suds but still some water is visible).

But now I want to show you how God loves and how he wants us to love. (Begin stirring vigorously so that the suds literally overflow the bowl and run down the sides). This is what happens when you put love into action. Do you see what happens when you try to love all of the time? There's more than enough for you and me and everybody else.

God's love is like soapsuds that are stirred up all the time. There's more love than we can ever use, but that's the way he is and that's the way he wants us to be.

JUMPING TO CONCLUSIONS

December

I Corinthians 4:5a "Be careful not to jump to conclusions before the Lord returns as to whether someone is a good servant or not."

Object: Any optical illusion, such as two lines drawn like this ⟵―――⟶ ⟶―――⟵ Notice that the lines are the same length, but arrows on the ends make the bottom line look longer.

Good morning, boys and girls. I wonder why I always say "good morning?" Maybe some Sunday I should say BAD SUNDAY, boys and girls. No, regardless of the weather or anything else it is always good to be in God's house.

Look at what I have here this morning. (Show them the optical illusion and ask them questions about it, such as which line is the longest? How can you tell? Would you like to measure them with a ruler -- or whatever is appropriate to reveal that it is an optical illusion. I might suggest contacting an optometrist for securing a good one for you.) It's strange how our eyes can fool us. Most of the time our eyes are such good friends that we believe whatever we see. But it isn't always true. Sometimes they tell us one thing when really something else is true.

I suppose people are sometimes like our optical illusion. We can never really be sure what is in their hearts. Maybe they are really happy even when they are crying or sad when they are laughing. Maybe they don't want to be alone even when it seems that they don't want friends.

Did you know that Saint Paul wrote in his letter to the Corinthians that God had told him to tell others that they should never jump to a conclusion about someone, as to whether he is good or bad? Our first impressions of some people might not be correct. Sometimes our hearts and our minds play funny tricks on us just like our eyes.

Do you know what I mean? Never say you dislike someone after just meeting him the first time. You never can tell but what the person whom you think you dislike may turn out to be your best friend.

What we should always do is look at the stranger like Jesus would and love him because he is one of God's children. If you do that you are not only being a Christian but you are showing others how a Christian should be.

WHY WE WORSHIP TOGETHER

Second Sunday in Advent　　　　　　　　　　　　　**December**

Romans 15:6　　　"And then all of us can praise the Lord together with one voice, giving glory to God, the Father of our Lord Jesus Christ."

Object:　　　　　Tape recorder

Good morning, boys and girls, and how are you on God's day? Do you know that sometimes I can hardly wait to get here on Sunday morning and see your bright faces? That's right. I can hardly wait. Now let's see what I have here today. Do you know what this is? (Hold up or point to tape recorder.) A tape recorder, that's right. And do you know what we do with a tape recorder? (Let several answer -- record music, voices, speeches.) How many of you would like to have your voice recorded on this tape? All of you? That's wonderful. O.K., why don't you just begin to talk, maybe you can say a poem that you know or sing a song, or laugh or talk to your friend sitting next to you, and I'll turn on the microphone and see what we get. (When you are getting quite a bit of talk and confusion you can turn it off.) Well, now, that was great because I can take this home and listen to it and I will know just who it was that spoke and I will always...Oh, you want to hear it now? Right now? O.K. Let's play it back. (Turn it on and let it play until you can hear nothing but confusion.) Oh my, I will never figure out what was being said, let alone distinguish the voices. Let me try again. Only this time I want to hear what is being said. Let's practice saying one thing all together, like "Praise God." Can you all say that? "Praise God." One more time and let's say it slowly and distinctly and not shout. O.K.? "Praise God."

Wonderful! Now let's try it just like that for the tape recorder. (Play again but notice where you are starting the tape so they can hear the contrast between the confused voices and the unison statement, "Praise God"). That's good! Now let's play it back.

Now you understand why we want to worship together by singing the same songs and praying the same prayer and listening to the same Bible passage. See how much more we can get done when we work and worship together. Christians want God to know that they are worshipping together because then there is less confusion. You and I ought to remember what we learned from the tape recorder. We can do best and learn best when we do it together.

BLUEPRINT FOR ACTION

                              December

Romans 13:14   "But ask the Lord Jesus Christ to help you live as you should and don't make plans to enjoy evil." (Taken from Paraprashed Epistles of Living Letters.)

Object: **Blueprint**

Good morning, boys and girls; or maybe I should say Happy New Year. Happy New Year? Did you know that according to the church calendar this is the first day of the church year? That's right. We call it Advent and it means to prepare or get ready for the Savior's coming. Do you know what I like best about preparing? I like the idea of making a plan! How many of you like to make plans?

I have a very special plan here this morning. (Take out blueprint -- hold it up and let them tell you what it is.) Do you know what this is? A blueprint -- that's right. Do you know what kind of men use blueprints? (Again let them guess -- carpenters, plumbers, etc.) Right. Do any of your daddies work with blueprints? They do?

Now when you have a blueprint you have a plan and that plan tells you exactly what to do. It tells you how long to cut a board and where to nail it. It tells you where to put the light, how high to lay the bricks and you follow that plan and you get it done.

Now the Bible tells us today that there are two kinds of plans for life. One of those plans is called evil and when we plan to be evil or bad it's terrible. Do you remember when you planned to tell a lie or fight with your brother or sister? That's an evil plan and God doesn't like that. It makes us feel bad, and it hurts others as well.

Now the Bible says there is another plan, and that plan is the way Jesus taught us to live. When we plan to be like Jesus we always think of the kindest things to say, or do. It's like being nice to someone whose feelings were hurt or doing the dishes for mother without being asked or helping someone secretly without his ever guessing who it was who helped him.

There are two plans for life and God wants to know which plan you are going to follow. Is it the bad plan or is it the good one? Do you want to plan evil things or the things that Jesus asks you to do? I think I know which one you would choose.

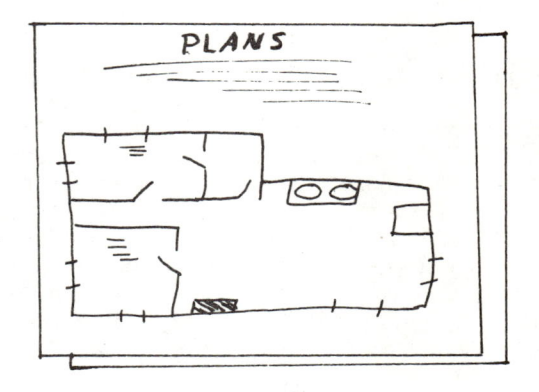

THE JOY OF GIVING

December

Philippians 4:5 — "Let everyone see that you are unselfish and gentle in all that you do."

Object: Candy (bars or little chocolate Santa Claus's) enough for each child.

Good morning children. Are you getting excited? Someone told me there was going to be a special day soon but I can't remember what it is. Christmas, that's right. Why do you like Christmas so much? (Here it is very important that you get someone or more than one to say they like Christmas because they get presents.) Because you get presents. How many of you remember the presents you got last year for Christmas? Let's all think real hard. What did you get last year? (As they recall one or two things ask them what else.) Can you remember any more? No? Well then, that must be all that you got. Some of you didn't receive any gifts last year because you can't remember them. Is that right?

Did any of you give anyone else a gift last year? Let's think and see if we can remember a gift that we gave away last year to someone we loved. (See how many can remember the gift they made at school -- pencil holder, pot holder, etc.) Who did you give it to? Wasn't that fun? How many of you like to give presents to people that you love? That's fine.

Did you know that Jesus was God's gift to us on the first Christmas? That's right. We didn't buy him, we didn't even ask for him but God gave him to us. Isn't that wonderful? Isn't that the best gift anyone ever got?

I like to give gifts to other people. I am going to give you a gift this morning, but there's a catch to it. Since you like to give gifts and I like to give gifts and I don't know who you want to give your gifts to, I have a plan.

How many of you like candy? How many of your friends like candy? I'm going to give you some special candy to give to your friend. That's right. I'll give you a piece of candy if you'll promise to give it to someone else and not eat it yourself.

Did you know that God wants us to be unselfish and to give what we have to others? He does, and he says that when we do it makes us feel good. (Distribute candy to all who promise to give it to someone else).

Just think how many of your friends are going to be happy today. When they ask why you are giving them the candy, you tell them because God gave us Jesus as a gift and he made us so happy, you want to make them happy too. O.K.?

God bless you and merry Christmas.

BEING IN GOD'S FAMILY

December

Galatians 4:7   "And since we are his sons, everything he has belongs to us, for that is the way God planned."

Object: Something that belongs to the entire family but was bought by the Father. (A picture of one of the youngsters' home, a sack of potatoes or some food. A picture of the family car. Someone with a Polaroid camera could take all of these in a few minutes.)

Good morning, boys and girls, and how are you today? Did you have an exciting Christmas? Did you help Jesus celebrate his birthday? I'm glad that you all had a great time. Jesus likes us to have fun on his birthday as well as to be thankful for his coming.

Well, now, let's see what I have for you today. First of all I have a picture. Does anyone know what that is? (Wait until the child who lives there says, "It's my house.") Your house! Well, isn't that wonderful! Let's see what else I have here. (Hold up picture of someone's car and wait until the child exclaims, "It's our car." This can be continued with a picture of a pet a school or church.)

Why do you keep saying that it is your house, your car, your dog, your school? Did you buy them? Do they really belong to you? Who bought them or helps to keep them going? Your Father and Mother. That's right. But you feel like they belong to you, don't you? You should because when your mom and dad moved into that house they moved in for you too. They bought that car for all of you and the pet is for the whole family. That is part of God's plan for families: that we all have and share together even if our fathers and mothers work hard to make money to buy it. It still belongs to us all.

Our families are like that because that is the same way God is with us. God makes the sun shine and the food to grow and the trees to give wood for our houses and the children for our families. Everything really belongs to God because he made it. But it also belongs to us because we are part of his family and he wants us to share it.

Isn't God a wonderful Father to let us all share in his beautiful world? He is never selfish and provides all the things we need.